The Filled Cup

3 Keys to Finding Breakthrough in Public Service Work

LISA HALEY

The Filled Cup
© 2022 Lisa Haley
www.TheFilledCup.info

Published with help from 100X Publishing
Olympia, Washington | www.100xPublishing.com

ISBN: 979-8-9872786-0-4

"Lisa Haley and I are colleagues in public finance and serve together on the board of the Virginia chapter of Women in Public Finance. Lisa is enthusiastic, full of energy and drive. She has creative ideas and goes to work to make them happen, as well as being a great communicator and serving well in a leadership role to accomplish action items and affect change. Lisa has led our VWPF's DEI Committee since its formation and can be credited with many of its accomplishments."

— Ann Shawver, Owner/Consultant of
Ann Harrity Shawver, CPA, PLLC

"Lisa Haley's new book offers a guide for how to achieve and stay in a mindset where we are doing our best work. Using humor and real-life examples of her own, she outlines the steps she found worked best to fill her own cup and shares her journey of discovery. Her ideas are delivered in concise, bite-size pieces that are easily understood, in a style that makes this book a quick and uplifting read. Everyone owes it to themselves to read *The Filled Cup: 3 Keys to Finding Breakthrough in Public Service Work.*"

— Tana Suter, International HR Consultant

"As the former Debt Manager of the City of Los Angeles, I managed a $6 billion portfolio. Lisa is an excellent coach and was always there to answer my questions and direct me to the right place to find answers. Lisa is an exceptional advocate for women in the public finance sector."

— Natalie Brill, Former Debt Manager,
City of Los Angeles, CA

Dedication:

Tim, I love you, and I thank God for you.
Thank you for choosing me, pursuing me, and taking
me on the adventure of my life.

Jared, Lydia, and Shelby, you are gifts from God.
I love you!

A friendly reminder that you are like a well, and a well without water is an empty hole in the ground.

Table of Contents

Introduction 9

Chapter 1: Fill Up Your Cup 17
Cup Filling Part 1 – Person

Chapter 2: Cup Filling Part 2 – Perspectives 35

Chapter 3: Cup Filling Part 3 – Professional Skills . . . 45

Chapter 4: Full Cup Service 53

The Filled Cup Self-Assessment 57

About the Author 59

Introduction

Public service is a high calling that touches every facet of our daily lives in significant ways. Without public service, our communities and way of life would cease to thrive. Work in public service ranges from agriculture, education, and emergency services, to healthcare, justice, consumer protection, transportation, and infrastructure. My ties to public service started before I was born, a legacy my father started by serving in the United States Army.

For me, his tour to Vietnam prior to my birth—earning a purple heart, his selfless sacrifice, and his example with 30 years of distinguished service to our country and our family—laid the ground work for all I hold dear in regard to excellence in service to others. In the early 1990s, I got an up close and personal front-row seat to his stellar service when I worked alongside my dad as contractor consulting for the federal government. I witnessed servanthood in action as he led his divisions and teams with the heart of a loving father. I will never forget how much his team respected and genuinely enjoyed working for and with him. He has been my inspiration, a true example to emulate because of his seemingly effortless and impactful style.

While working with him, I began to realize I enjoyed helping people and that I, too, had a desire to serve people and be a part of something bigger than myself. In 2004, my public service journey took me to the education field. When my children were in elementary school, I began working as a part-time preschool teacher. Working with toddlers is not for the faint of heart, as they say, but I did develop deep levels of gratitude for my own bundles of joy. There is nothing like working with other people's children to help you appreciate your own!

In those days, my customers were a very demanding bunch of three-year-olds, just learning to separate from their parents for a few hours a week. As with most jobs, including jobs in public service, some days were better than others. I guided, corrected, fed, hugged, cared for, and encouraged my pint-sized customers, and not surprisingly, issues came up. Such is life!

It was in that proving ground of privilege, while working alongside some very caring and dedicated teachers who modeled passionate service, when I learned the art dealing with extreme swings of emotion, dramatic escalation, and difficult to comprehend communication (better known as temper tantrums and meltdowns). I found out a lot about the human condition, and honestly, the power and necessity of prayer. After all, we are encouraged to "pray without ceasing," by the Apostle Paul in 1 Thessalonians 5:17.

We humans often have secret and not-so-secret fears, heart wounds, offenses, and inner struggles. Anger, jealousy, and a spirit of criticism and judgement can ooze out all over the place in spectacular fashion given the right combination of frustration and selfish desire. "The heart is deceitful above all things, and desperately wicked, who can know it?" says the prophet Jeremiah (Jeremiah 17:9). This is naturally the case for three-year-olds and, sadly, can be for adults as well.

After eight years of runny noses, scraped knees, tears, laughter, and unidentifiable crafts, I transitioned to full-time public service with my local town's government. It was an opportunity to utilize my undergraduate and master's degree training in business. Although I had invested ten years in developing skills for serving adults, I said yes to the opportunity to serve children for a season where my technical business skills were not the focus of the job: the posture of my heart for service was the focus. This experience ended up giving me a greater capacity to love and care while serving others, and I ended up connected to my purpose in deep and meaningful ways.

It didn't take long in my new role in local government to realize that a lot of what I experienced, encountered, and practiced at the preschool in terms of my service to small humans, prepared me for interactions with adults. The big humans, too, were not always happy about their situation and were more than happy to vocalize it on the nearest unsuspecting person. Unhappy adults can be prone to freely unloading their frustrations, feelings of being disrespected, or wronged on unsuspecting and undeserving public servants who happen to be in the right place at the wrong time. As they say, hurt people, hurt people.

The revelation that my time of service to three-year-olds at the preschool would give me such perspective and understanding —grace, really—in dealing with adults was not lost on me; it provided lessons of supreme value and worth. I truly appreciate the time of preparation for where I serve now. You may have heard it said, but it bears repeating, do not despise small beginnings. "For who has despised the day of small things?" as it says in Zechariah 4:10. I believe showing up and serving children with concern and care, despite having two degrees and technical training in business, opened the door to being trusted with a different assignment. It led to the great privilege and responsibility for my senior leadership role in my local government finance office where I am responsible for millions of our taxpayer dollars.

Wikipedia notes that public service is "any service intended to address specific needs pertaining to the aggregate members of a community."[1] While true, this definition sounds clinical and not very warm or fuzzy. According to Cambridge Dictionary, "public service is something done or provided to the public because it is needed..."[2] In other words, it's essential. Now we are getting somewhere.

Service is essential. Need is the fundamental catalyst behind the call to serve, but all too often those who answer the call are not held in very high regard. Instead of being celebrated for sacrificial service and dedication, those in public service are viewed as "nameless and faceless bureaucrats who are underworked and overpaid" per a 2014 Harvard Business Review article.[3] Ouch, that's a bit harsh! As recently as October 2022, an article in *Governing* opened with "It's a fact of life for public bureaucrats that they

[1]Wikipedia, c/o McGregor, Eugene B. Jr; Campbell, Alan; Macy, Anthony: Cleveland, Harlan (July-August 1982 "Symposium: The Public Service Institution". Public Administration Review. Washington. 42(4)304-320.
[2]Cambridge dictionary.org
[3] Harvard Business Review, Lavigna, Robert "Why Government Workers are Harder to Motivate" November 28, 2014.

almost never get noticed for the things they do, even when their work is spectacularly good or egregiously bad."[4] With this sentiment, it's no wonder the Brookings Institute found "appreciation of, and respect for public servants have steadily declined in the United States since the 1960s."[5] Clearly something is seriously wrong.

The negative perception that has existed for over 60 years has taken its toll on the public service workforce based on the Washington Post 2022 report on the declining employee engagement scores in government.[6] This perception and low levels of engagement have been the topic of many studies, and the recent pandemic of 2020 has only created more stress and strain on an already beleaguered segment of workers.

Despite all the negativity, and contrary to what one may read on the internet, hear on the news from politicians, or from customer feedback, there is honor, dignity, and excellence in public service by those who deliver it. A less-than-glowing perception can be flipped on its head if you are willing to set yourself

---

[4] Governing, Ehrenhalt, Alan, "A Government Fixer's Tricks of the Trade", October 12, 2022.
[5] Brookings.edu, Hill, Fiona, "Public service and the federal government" May 27, 2020.
[6] washingtonpost.com Davidson, Joe, "Federal employees are not happy. These agencies are especially troubled" July 13, 2020.

apart through the way in which you serve. You may not alter 60 years of low-bar service perception overnight, but you can do what you can with what you have today!

All of us are keenly aware of the positive effects of receiving outstanding service; it brightens our day and lightens our load, helping us believe there is hope in our fellow man. This same rare, highly achievable, and rewarding aim should be the basis of how we operate as we pour ourselves into serving the public. What we do can make a difference, and we can write a new ending to what up to now has been a sad story.

In the pages that follow, it's my hearts 'desire to share insights and experiences from my more than 15 years of public service, and hopefully a few laughs, that will remind, encourage, and inspire you to remember that public service is worthwhile, deeply rewarding, and valuable, but most importantly when delivered with great care, it will not only set you apart, but will set you up to be fulfilled and make lasting impact.

Meaningful public service with lasting impact is built upon a foundation of serving with excellence every day. Distinguished service requires your cup to be full, because just like a well without water is an empty hole in the ground, so, too, are you if you are serving others out of an empty cup. This book unlocks the actionable framework I have developed and used to propel me in my public service journey, and I know this framework will lead you to service excellence breakthrough.

Are you a woman in a public service role with a desire to serve well, yet find yourself feeling underappreciated, unfulfilled, or lacking influence and true impact? It's time to discover the keys to The Filled Cup Framework and transform your service delivery from run-of-the-mill to renown.

Chapter 1

Fill Up Your Cup

The actionable framework to service excellence is called The Filled Cup Framework (TFC). It's actionable because if you take consistent action over time, you can achieve transformation. If you invest in yourself and purpose to act, you will yield results. The decision is yours. In the words of Yoda, "Do or do not, there is not try."

Person

Perspective **Professional Skills**

TFC has three components, similar to the way an

equilateral triangle has three points and three equal sides. Cup filling is centered on the 3Ps of Person, Perspective, and Professional Skills.

Let's take a journey and discover the details in the chapters that follow. Here in Chapter One, we'll start with the first P: Person.

Cup Filling Part 1 - Person

Going back to the well analogy, usually water drawn from a well is put in a vessel for future use. You, my friend, are the vessel (or cup) who pours out into others through your service. A full cup starts with you, *the person*. Being a woman of deep faith, if you will indulge me, and without getting super spiritual or hung up on religiousness, can I give it to you straight? We, the people of planet earth, are uniquely created as body, soul, and spirit. The body is our physical flesh, bones, and organs. Our soul is the seat of our emotions, will, and mind. Our spirit can be thought of as our conscience, or our internal sense of right and wrong. This truth is what sets us apart as human beings from all other species.

When there is centeredness in our body, soul, and spirit, we have a greater probability to perform like a well-oiled machine. Centeredness or alignment in our person stems from who we are, and who we say we want to be, act, and interact with others. We often see examples of this in the successes of professional athletes, teams, and titans of industry at the top of their game. They set goals of being the best and take the steps to reach the top.

Conversely, when your *person* is out of alignment, you can function well for a time, but in reality you are operating on borrowed time. Like ignoring a check engine light in your car, you are inevitably heading for an expensive repair and inconvenient, unscheduled downtime.

We can see an example of this in the meteoric rise and tragic fall of Tiger Woods, whose personal life was out of balance, and it ultimately adversely impacted his professional career. At the time of his very public indiscretions, he had won 14 major championships and was on pace to eclipse Jack Nicholas' record of 18 major championships. On the surface it appeared he had mastered championship form. Instead, he endured an embarrassing and painful end to his marriage and position as a golf role model and icon. It took another decade for him to win another major championship when he won the 2019 Masters.[7] There is strong evidence that his *person* was out of alignment.

---

[7] USA Today.com, Peter, Josh, 10 years after Tiger Woods' crash: Untold stories of some connected to Woods' scandal, November 26, 2019.

CCFs

I like to think of a lack of alignment as a precursor to cracks, chips, and fissures, or CCFs, in our cup. They represent a threat to the structural integrity of our cup and our ability to serve well. Structural integrity is "the ability of a structure to withstand its intended loading without failing due to fracture, deformation, or fatigue."[8] CCFs can provide an avenue for undue seepage from our cup, leading to a possible blowout. A blowout is something we want to and can work to avoid.

You may agree that alignment sounds good, but you may be wondering *alignment with what?* Another truth is that we all align with something. We either attempt to align with other people, looking to them as the model to copy, as means for validation, or for how we think we should conduct ourselves. Sometimes these are sports heroes, internet influencers, high-level businesspeople, pastors, government officials, or other role models of notoriety, or we may even look to ourselves.

For me, I chose to align myself with the living Lord

---

[8] wikipedia.org

Jesus and His Word, the Bible, which is a guidebook for living. I tried the putting myself on the throne of my life before I accepted Jesus as Lord, but that result was lacking and empty on many levels. Deep down I had a longing that was only filled through surrendering my life to him, and building a relationship with him, as you do with a close friend. I abdicated the throne of my life and gave it to Jesus so he could live through me. "For none of us lives to himself..." (Romans 14:7), and God has a plan for my life and yours. "For I know the plans I have for you," declares the LORD, "plans to prosper you and not harm you, plans to give you hope and a future" (Jeremiah 29:11).

Surrendering my life was freeing and began to reveal my purpose; it pointed me to fulfillment. This is not to say that difficulties or pain or disappointment are no longer my reality. They are still a part of life, they just don't hold the power over me and my perspectives that they once did. As Jesus noted in John 16:33, "In this world you will have trouble. But take heart! I have overcome the world." Thankfully, I don't have to have all the answers, and I choose to rely on faith in him to face each day. "As you do not know the path of the wind, or how the body is formed in a mother's womb, so you cannot understand the work of God..." (Ecclesiastes 11:5). What about you? Who are you aligned with? What is your faith in?

Person – Body

As for the body, we only get one, so I recommend we treasure it and treat it well. Put in the right mix of fuel and rest, and you can put it through its paces. Choose to cut corners, and your body will surely communicate to you, usually in its own special way. If we are willing to listen, it will let us know we're off course. "He who has ears to hear, let him hear," Matthew 11:15 says.

Sometimes, this is easier said than done, I agree, but can I challenge you to take a moment and assess yourself for yourself? Are you out of alignment related to what you eat or with your relationship with food? Are you getting some physical activity and rest on a regular basis? Food is fuel. I love to eat. To me, it's one of the seven wonders of the world. Okay, so that would make it the 8th wonder...but who is counting? Let's face it, every good and perfect gift comes from above (James 1:17), including fried chicken, mac and cheese, and pie!

Another aspect of the human condition I have discovered over the years, or at least about my own condition, is our tendency toward extremes. At times, I've lived by the motto *all in or not at all*. I'm either in the deep end of the pool or I'm not even at the pool.

Spoiler alert: at its core, this life motto is not a position of being centered or aligned. I'm all too familiar with operating in a state of extremes. Moderating can be an area of struggle at times, and I have to be wildly intentional in my efforts to stay neutral. Yep, I have some CCFs in my cup that occasionally need my attention, such as my tendency to eat all the cookies in a batch! Somehow, my "extreme logic" thinks it makes sense to eat them all so that any temptation in the coming days will be removed; I can demonstrate my ability to cut out all sweets and sugar for stretches of time only to end up consuming more sugar than anyone ever should. Hmm...

Got Blind Spots?

If I fail to properly moderate, I can get sideswiped by a blind spot and end up way out of alignment. A blind spot is "an area where a person's view is obstructed." [9] In relation to my *person*, it is a character flaw that is visible to others yet out of my line of sight or awareness.

> **"Heart wounds create blind spots."**
> —Pedro Adao, Founder of 100X, 8-Figure

---

[9] Google's English dictionary by Oxford Languages

With a blind spot, the key is recognition and then addressing it before it's a full-blown problem that can steer you away from being who you say you want to be. Does your car have the lane monitoring feature that alerts you when another vehicle is in the lane next to you? It keeps you safe from a possible crash, and so does recognition, awareness, and addressing your blind spots; it keeps you from shattering your cup into a million pieces.

Recognition and change is good, but I am not suggesting you make a bunch of changes all at once. We do well to focus on one thing at a time. This is the crawl, walk, run concept. Multitasking is an elusive unicorn; it results in divided attention and *less than* results. Take a single action. Seeing success with one action helps to create confidence that you can achieve sustainable momentum.

As you read these words, do you feel a nudge about something related to how you view or use food or how you need to move your body for your health or rest? If so, can you come up with a single action to implement? Let me encourage you to invest in you. Your greatest gain will come from your decision to take action, act, and move towards being consistent with what you say you want. My friend, are you ready?

Person – Emotions

Our emotions are an interesting and tricky part of who we are, who we want to be, and how we interact in the world around us. Maybe you've noticed this too. Clearly, positive emotions such as laughter and excitement bring joy to life.

"A cheerful disposition is good for your health."
—Proverbs 17:22 (MSG)

I have such appreciation for the importance of laughter, now more than ever. When our children were small, their giggles and genuine childlike excitement over the seemingly trivial things—like fireflies lighting up a warm summer night, seeing a rainbow in the sky after a rain storm, squeals of delight for the gift of no school on a snow day—were truly heartwarming. It was a great reminder to me to lighten up, as sometimes I can be way too serious. Life is short; it doesn't have to be so weighty all the time, and I find laughter is a big help.

As my number of days on the planet and gray hairs on my head continue to grow, my husband and I keep humor at the core of our relationship. While we aren't tech wizards, we navigate empty nesting by text bombing each other humorous internet memes and videos to keep the joy and laughter flowing in our everyday lives. From Gru's Minions to Grogu (aka Baby

Yoda), our texts are sometimes corny, sometimes goofy, but always good for a hearty laugh. A hearty laugh is often the welcomed bright spot to any day.

Our emotions, much like our *person*, benefit from being centered or aligned. Extremes are dangerous in either direction, high or low. These stark poles can be a definitive opening to unwanted cracks, chips, and fissures. Sometimes, life experiences like lack of sleep, fear, anxiety, or grief can exert undue influence on our emotions. They can lead us to a one-way ride on the struggle bus, hindering healthy expression of them, or they can end up controlling and leading us with unintended harmful consequences.

There are times in life when we may need to raise our hand and say, "I am not okay." There is no shame in it. Actually, there is freeing power in calling it what it is. In fact, it is the bravest admittance of all. According to Adam Grant, science author and professor at Wharton School, University of Pennsylvania, "Too many people wait until they're exhausted or depressed to make change or seek help." Personally, I know this to be true.

Seeing a Blind Spot

Not long ago, I came face to face with a blind spot of mine causing serious friction in my marriage. Over my 27 years of wedded bliss (sometimes short on the bliss part), I hit my head on the figurative door frame of poor communication with my spouse for the umpteenth time. It is well known in my family I am slow at recognizing patterns, and this communication struggle was no different. I seem to excel in communicating at work but somehow epically fail sometimes with the ones I love so dearly, especially my husband.

Things got so untenable in the winter of 2022, that I sought out counseling through my local church at the urging of a trusted friend. I could have tried to play the blame game or rationalize the issue as male/female style differences, but I knew better.

After some self-reflection, I correctly concluded that what I really wanted more than anything was harmony in our relationship; there were steps I could take to move toward improving our communication, but I needed help to understand how I could achieve it.

"If it is possible, as much as it depends on you,
live peaceably with all men."
—Romans 12:18

I don't really recall what I thought counseling would be, but it wasn't at all what I expected. It allowed me a safe space to articulate what I was experiencing and feeling and receive unbiased input and gentle truth to course correct some things I have struggled to execute well in my marriage. There is value in not doing life alone. I am a work in progress, and progress is developing because of a cry for help, a decision, and action. Change is a process, and we must trust the process. Be willing to not only consider change, but press in to change even where it may be uncomfortable and messy.

To master service excellence, we need deep understanding of the power of emotions in ourselves so we can understand others. This understanding of ourselves should be a beacon of insight to us as we serve others. If emotions are a shared human trait, and they most assuredly are, it is critical to be a subject matter expert. Proverbs 16:16 says, "How much better to get wisdom than gold! And to get understanding is to be chosen rather than silver."

While serving, it's possible you may encounter a boss, coworker, or customer in the throes of emotional turmoil who needs an extra measure of your grace and empathy. Keeping this in the forefront of your mind while working, shopping, or interacting with family and friends is where it all starts.

For me personally, I lean on this regularly; I recognize I have been the recipient of my share of unmerited grace and empathy many times in my five decades. Yogi Bhajan framed it well when he said, "If you are willing to look at another person's behavior toward you as a reflection of the state of their relationship with themselves rather than a statement about your value as a person, then you will, over a period of time cease to react at all." Situations sometimes are not as they seem on the surface...if we take the time to understand.

If you think you may need help or want to go deeper in understanding your emotions and their impacts in your life and on others, you may want to enlist support from a licensed professional. The point here is to acknowledge we have emotions, they sometimes get the best of us, and we need to monitor them for warning signs that something may need attention.

Person – Spirit

The last part of your *person* is your spirit. Merriam-Webster defines it as "the sense or consciousness of the moral goodness or blameworthiness of one's own conduct, intentions, or character together with a feeling of obligation to do right or be good."[10] It's the still, small voice that acts as our moral center.

Alignment for this element of our *person* looks more

---

[10] merriam-webster.com

like listening to and acting upon the internal promptings instead of ignoring them. In 2012, I had just begun competing in sprint triathlons—a race with swimming, biking, and running—as a weekend warrior. I like a good challenge, so why not three at once? I had completed the Tri-Rock triathlon race in Annapolis, Maryland, and was going out for easy run the week after the event. I normally went for runs without my phone on the back roads in the rural area where we lived at the time. That day, I distinctly remember feeling a strong urging to take my phone. I thought it was so peculiar but blithely chose to ignore it, and off I went on my merry way without it.

We had a hill on the run route that I affectionately named "heartbreak hill," as it was quite steep and would break my heart as I gasped for air trying to run it. As runners know, for every uphill, there is an equal and opposite downhill. The downhill for heartbreak was a twisting, curvy, unpaved, blind decent.

As I made my way down, I heard a sound that made my heart go into full panic: a meek cry for help. A car had careened off the road, flipped over in a small creek bed at the base of the hill, and apparently a driver was trapped and calling for help. I can't tell you how many times I had taken that same road (admittedly too fast) when driving but escaped unscathed.

I am sad to say that this day was not my finest hour and is a great example of being out of alignment to the prompting of my inner spirit. I tend to be panic-stricken in emergency situations, which is one of the many reasons I have the highest respect for first responders. My flight mechanism was in overdrive, and I took off running up the next hill, away from the over-turned car, as though I had been shot out of a cannon from fright. Feeling bad and scared, I ran to the nearest house for help, which wasn't that near. Someone finally answered the door, and between pants I explained what I encountered.

The neighbor, much calmer than I, called 9-1-1 and sprang into action. We went back to the site of the crash, and without hesitation, she crawled into the creek down to the car. To our shock, the person was no longer there. Apparently, during the time I fled the scene, the injured driver dislodged themselves and went up hill the other way to get actual help...not inaction from a frightened, unhelpful passerby. Despite my inaction, I'm thankful all things worked out in the end.

In the words of the grail knight in *Indiana Jones and the Last Crusade*, "I chose poorly," and ignored the nudge to take my phone. Worse yet, I failed to answer the call to help serve someone in need. To this day, I cringe at the thought of how I handled this, and I used to beat myself up over it. Had my person been an actual cup, it would have been smashed to bits. Forensics would have found no evidence of CCFs because the destruction was so great. Not only did I have to forgive myself for being such a chicken and an awful Samaritan, I've had to learn to heed and act on the promptings from within. These promptings can situate you to be a source of help or protection for you and others.

Lessons Learned – Heed the Promptings

Thankfully, this moment of failure was a moment in time, not my final destination. Fast forward to the months after adjusting to the pandemic: we returned to in-office work on varying schedules. While on a walk during my lunch break, I passed a woman unloading her vehicle to contribute donations to the victims of the war in Ukraine. I remember thinking as I passed, "Wow, she has quite a few donations." No sooner had this thought entered my mind while passing her did I feel the familiar urge, along with a sort of whisper in my mind: *You help her.* I literally stopped in my tracks on the sidewalk.

After a mini tug of war with the thoughts in my mind, I turned around, approached her car, and asked her if she needed help; the donation box was a good distance away inside Town Hall. She took me up on my offer, and I proceeded to show her where to go. After a brief chat, we said our goodbyes and I went on to finish my walk. I felt pretty sure I experienced what scientists have termed "helpers high," which is where "altruistic behavior releases endorphins in the brain, producing the positive feeling[11].

Interestingly, science has confirmed words of truth spoken long ago. After all, Jesus said, "It's more blessed to give than receive" (Acts 20:35). Granted, this was not a life-and-limb moment like the heartbreak hill debacle, but a yes to your conscience when prompted not only brings joy and serves others, but it fills you too.

Now we have an understanding of the first element of the 3P Framework: your *person*. Your *person* is the integration of your body, soul, and spirit – getting a handle on our emotions, listening to our still small voice, and watching out for blind spots, and knowing when to ask for and seek help.

Next up in the framework, let's discuss *perspective*.

[11] Suttie, Jill; Marsh, Jason, Greater Good Magazine, University of California - Berkley, December 13, 2010

Chapter 2

Cup Filling Part 2 - Perspective

People are as unique as the number of grains of sand at my favorite beach, Emerald Isle, North Carolina. At Emerald Isle, you encounter many different types of people, from locals who work the vacation rental properties, fishermen who work the sea, and natives, to transplants, seasonal workers, and tourists. One of my favorites is the fishmonger who sells fresh scallops with a smile and story. The variety of people found at the beach adds to the uniqueness of my visits and makes the trips interesting and memorable.

A key by-product of uniqueness is differing perspectives. Perspective is the second concept in The Filled Cup Framework. Perspective is "a particular attitude toward or way of regarding something; a point of view."[12] As discussed in Chapter One, our soul is directly influenced and impacted by our mind.

"Heaven and earth intersect in our mind."

---

[12] Google's English Dictionary by Oxford Languages.

— Lysa Terkeurst, American Speaker and New York
Times Bestselling Author

Similar to how our *person* needs to be in alignment to excel in serving, our perspectives drive how we approach and deliver our service to others. Our mind is the filter for our thoughts and perspectives, and they are molded, shaped, and influenced by a myriad of factors including our words. "Death and life are in the power of the tongue" (Proverbs 18:21).

We process words and speak words every day, all day long, to ourselves and others. If you lean extrovert, as you may have guessed I do, you may share some 8,000 words a day; introverts offer half that, around 4,000 words. Women in general average 20,000 words a day, according to the internet. The inside joke in my house with my introverted spouse is that at dinner, I can tell if he has "used up" all his words during the day. Low levels of desire to communicate after a long day are an indication. I have learned to take the opportunity to show grace and empathy in moments like these.

Whether we are thinking or speaking them, our words matter; they are inextricably linked to our thoughts and perspectives, as illustrated by this poem from an unknown author:

Your mind is a garden

Your thoughts are the seeds.
You can grow flowers
Or you can grow weeds.

The flowers or weeds are the result of our choices. To keep the weeds at bay in the garden of my mind, and ultimately what is influencing and shaping my thoughts and perspectives, I have to be intentional and conscious of the content I consume. Garbage in, garbage out.

"For out of the abundance of the heart
the mouth speaks."
—Matthew 12:34

"But those things which proceed out of the
mouth come from the heart."
—Matthew 15:18

There is a critical connection between thoughts in our minds and condition of our hearts.

Don't Overdo It

In recent years, I have embraced the value of news and social media content, but I have greatly cut back on my consumption of it, as well as being conscious of the time of day I consume it. I have found that how I feel about who I am and who I say I want to be is constantly under the influence of what I allow into my mind.

Generally, I do not read or view the news first or last thing in a day, and I do so in smaller doses from multiple sources and vantage points. Contrast this with consuming two to three hours of televised news programming in a single sitting. While it is important to know what's going on in the world, it takes effort to guard against the messages of negativity; negative messages can be a source of stress, strife, and fear in our hearts and minds. Moderating my news consumption also frees me for time for other pursuits and things I enjoy.

I also have to be vigilant to limit my social media consumption. You may be thinking this is too extreme and rigid. It may be, but as I already mentioned, I can struggle to do things in moderation. Setting limits can be an incredible anecdote to an area that might need some boundaries.

During the reporting of 9/11, I remember being glued to the television for days. The tragedy was important information, yet I struggled to limit where and how much of it I consumed. (Queue the CCFs in my cup.) It took the nudge of a loving spouse to remind me to step away from it, as we had small children who were getting over saturated with the amount of news coverage I was constantly viewing; they did not need exposure to it due to my inability to look away. It was like a car accident on the interstate: every passerby creates a bottle neck as they slow to survey the accident scene.

News is supposed to provide "a utility to empower the informed."[13] A lot of news today is fear-based, trying to grab your attention as a teaser, promising the solution within the story. It's known as the "if it bleeds, it leads" programming.[14] Content has the potential to have great sway over our perspectives and our service. How? Because it can fuel limiting beliefs or create and reinforce victim mentalities that short circuit the excellence in our service. I am not suggesting to shove your head in the sand like an ostrich. By all means, no!

Instead, do an assessment of your content consumption. Do you overdo it with consuming news, social media, or other programming, from sports to home decorating? Does the thought of separating from your streaming service or smartphone for a time in order to focus intently or be overtly present make you uneasy? Healthy perspectives, including monitoring and filtering the content we consume, are not just unicorns and rainbows; they have real power to allow

---

[13] American Press Institute, "What is the purpose of journalism?" October 6, 2022
[14] Serene, Deborah, Psychology Today, "If It Bleeds, It Leads: Understanding Fear-Based Media, June 7, 2011.

our minds (and ultimately our service) to be wielded for good...the greater good.

Position

Part of the power in perspective stems from position. Our position, or heart posture, when we serve tends to be either one of hubris or humility. We have all seen hubris in action: the wielding of excessive pride or arrogance. CCFs are on full display when a position of hubris is present. It's ultimately a mask for an unrecognized blind spot that can lead to collapse. Jesus addressed this: "For whoever exalts himself will be humbled, and he who humbles himself will be exalted" (Luke 14:11).

Unfortunately, in instances of public service, there can be displays of hubris where a boss, coworker, or customer is demanding and belittling, feeling justified under the banner of *the customer is always right*. The antidote to hubris is humility, and it is aided by a proper view of oneself, as the Apostle Paul reminds us in Romans 12:3: "...not to think of oneself more highly than he ought..." Humility is the view of others being greater than yourself.

**"But he who is greatest among you
shall be your servant."**

Throughout history, there are many examples of humility in service, from the care and concern of Mother Theresa for the poor and indigent, to the American heroes on United Airlines flight 93 on 9/11 who led with the "Let's Roll" motto to take down the terrorist hijackers who had overtaken their plane. Ultimately, the plane crashed near Shanksville, Pennsylvania, and all perished for the greater good.

Perspective has, at its core, a decision. An attitude, or point of view, is the conclusion drawn or result of a decision to think a particular way or to hold fast to a particular point of view. Our most effective decisions come from a proper perspective. Why? Because proper perspectives dismiss presumption; they hinge on comprehensive information assimilation and understanding. Sometimes this needs to occur in compressed moments of time, like when serving the public. The difficulty lies in the fact that we come with predisposed views and bias that can hinder our ability to process neutrally and thoroughly.

Perspective is a skill to master for service excellence. It's why automobile mechanics put cars on a lift to perform a repair. With the vehicle on the ground, the vantage point is limited, making it difficult to assess what is needed. Once perspective is achieved, the opportunity to model and offer grace can propel you to next-level service. Grace, in one spiritual definition, is getting what you don't deserve. It is unmerited favor we receive when we would should not receive it. Examples of grace can be seen when you get a warning for speeding instead of at ticket, you offer kindness in your service to someone who is unkind, or when you choose to forgive someone who has wronged you in a relationship.

The Summit

Over the Fourth of July weekend in 2022, we visited Pike's Peak National Park near Colorado Springs, Colorado. From miles away on our way to the park, Pike's Peak stood majestically in the distance. Once inside the park, we drove for 16 miles on a twisting, turning road with mountain goats and trees (sometimes without guardrails), taking in wildly beautiful scenery. At times, my perception of the massive mountain range was blocked or skewed. Finally, we arrived at the shuttle landing area with only three miles to go to reach the summit. The air was thinning, and my senses were buffeted from the temperature drop from the base temperature of 80 degrees to 65 degrees as we climbed higher.

Two months prior to visiting Pike's Peak, I had been working in Santa Fe, New Mexico, which has an elevation of 7,298 feet and felt I was accustomed to high altitudes. To my surprise, the altitude at the shuttle landing was dizzying, and we still had three miles to go. My hubris and poor assumptions were quickly dismantled at the higher elevations. The CCFs in my cup were erupting like an active volcano in the Hawaiian Islands because I was so misinformed on all counts.

We boarded the shuttle and made the summit, where the elevation is 14,115 feet, otherwise known as a "14er" to the climbing savvy. More than double the elevation of anything I had experienced before, the height difference was unmistakable. I will never forget how incredibly beautiful the unobstructed view at the summit was and how far we could see. Breckenridge's mountain range was visible, which was over 100 miles away.

I was struck by a comment from our shuttle driver about how the conditions at the summit can very quickly go from clear as bell to no visibility. It's similar to when we are trying to navigate issues and situations. We need clear and complete visibility to have the right perspective and proper approach. Ultimately, we make better decisions when we have perspective, and better perspective results in better service.

Our thoughts and perspectives impact our attitude and

our actions. We all encounter difficult people or situations from time to time. The question is, how are you going respond and show up in those moments? Our response reveals our character and blind spots. Is it possible that you have the power to reframe what you see, how you see it, and how you choose to act? What if you stop to ask what the situation is revealing instead of jumping to pre-rehearsed conclusions? What if the situation is happening for you not to you?

In the words of Maya Angelo, "If you can't change it, change your attitude." In some cases, you have to change your bad-ttitude. I have a tendency to be a bit on the impulsive side, quick with a comment or rebuttal, where my spouse is more thoughtful and measured. Let me share an example...

My Way?

When our son had one year left to complete his college degree, he informed his father and I that he was taking a gap year. My reaction failed to demonstrate any measure of comprehensive perspective. I tend to have more of a pull-up-your-boot-straps type of response to stress and difficulty, so I couldn't fathom why he would pause so close to completing his studies. I quickly told him as much, somewhat repeatedly, and without any proper reflection on the possibility that I was lacking perspective. My CCFs were coming fast and furious. Deep down, I somehow thought my way was the best and only way, and his decision to step away from college for a year reflected poorly on me (when it had nothing to do with me). Oh the arrogance of it all! My pride put such unnecessary strain and pain in my relationship with my son.

"By pride comes nothing but strife..."
Proverbs 13:10

He felt burnt out and needed a break, and I failed to serve my son because of my inability to see differently and truly try to understand. My immediate response could have been compassion and grace, but it was a blind spot of epic proportion.

While I started supporting his decision with my words, I was slow to internalize what he was feeling or why it made sense for him to take a break. I continued to make it about me. Unfortunately, it took many heated conversations and arguments that I genuinely regret. If I'm being honest, it also took more time than I prefer to admit to get to the realization that not only did he know he needed a break—a healthy response to overload—but that it *was* the right, best thing for him at the time.

It wasn't until he had returned to school a year later and was about to graduate when I could see the benefits of his break on his *person*. I finally got the perspective that was so elusive earlier. It wasn't about me. In hindsight, I eventually got clarity and peace. I did ask my son for forgiveness and admitted I was wrong, and in so doing strengthened our relationship and rebuilt what I tore down.

Take a moment and reflect; do you have a relationship that needs greater perspective on a matter and perhaps an apology? Make a decision and choose a path to improved perspective and restored relationship.

"Two roads diverged in a wood, and I took the one less traveled and that has made all the difference."
Robert Frost, *The Road Not Taken*

The gap year remains a very tangible reminder that I don't know it all, and better yet, a more comprehensive perspective leads to better decisions and better service. The power is in your perspective, even if it is slow in coming.

As we close this chapter on perspective, here's a quick summary. Part two of the 3Ps in The Filled Cup Framework is perspective, which is impacted by:

- the words we use and think
- the content we consume and are influenced by
- the position of our heart

- whether we choose hubris or humility and how it impacts the decisions we make
- our choice to offer grace as we pour ourselves out in service to others

Chapter 3

Cup Filling Part 3 – Professional Skills

The third and final element in the 3Ps of The Filled Cup Framework is your professional skills. Think of your person and perspective as inward facing, while your professional skills face out. They are a mix of what the world sees in you and what you bring as an offer of service.

Assessment of where your skills are now, where you want them to be, and how to level them up is a crucial step to this third part of the framework. This requires taking stock. Your current skills are the result of investments you have made in yourself and fall into two broad categories: technical and soft. You most likely have a solid foundation from the current position or role you occupy. You may be just starting out with a new organization or you may have had your role for decades. In either case, think about what you know about what you do.

You've Got Skills

You either gained the skills through prior work experience, repetition and mastery, higher education, completed a training program, or picked it up through trial and error. All the ways in which you have learned, practiced, collaborated, made mistakes, pointed out pitfalls or problems, and taught others elements of your job are part of your technical skill set. Often we don't give ourselves enough credit for what we actually do know about what we do...or how well we do it.

Soft skills are also essential; they're the ways in which you interact with team members and customers, how you handle stressful encounters, and the method in which you communicate. These categories all point to your relational skill set and can either boost or hinder your service.

Both technical and soft skills are vital to next-level service. Next-level service requires preparation and time. The skills you build day in and day out are part of your tool box, and paired with your person and perspective from the first two chapters, are the keys to propel your service toward consistent excellence. Where you want your skills to be and take you hinges on your willingness to choose to grow. We grow the most through discomfort and trial.

Imagine the change that takes place when a pot of boiling water hardens an egg or softens a potato. The boiling water is the catalyst which alters the state of the egg or potato. The potential CCFs in the professional skills area of your cup being full are tied to a "fixed mindset." A fixed mindset, if we are honest, can be like a comfortable go-to pair of sweatpants. We will pull those on every time we're given the chance! So, a fixed mindset is any unwillingness or resistance to try something new or welcome change.

I ride bikes for fitness and fun. Occasionally I participate in road bike races as part of my weekend warrior pursuits to stay active and healthy. I have been successfully riding bicycles for the better part of 50 years. When I say *successfully*, I mean to say I can pedal my bike and ride without crashing…although I have had a crash or two over the years. To pedal a bicycle, you simply push on the pedals in alternating circles with each of your legs to provide power. Not exactly brain surgery, right?

Another Way

It wasn't until this past summer of 2022 when I heard a cycling coach on the internet explain, in less than five minutes, the actual mechanics of the pedal stroke. I had been doing it wrong for 50 years! I had no idea there were actual mechanics to your pedal stroke. I mean, don't you just push the pedal by alternating your legs to provide power? Well, yes and no. While I was able to ride my bike and pedal, there was a better way.

I don't remember anyone ever explaining "how" to pedal in a way that improved my efficiency so dramatically. To my wonder, amazement, and (full disclosure) embarrassment, this simple explanation opened up a whole new level of speed and ease to my cycling. I struggled unnecessarily for years, stuck in bad habits due to poor information and no real catalyst to change.

You might be saying *what does this have to do with professional skills?* I was clearly stuck in my ways, pedaling incorrectly for 50 years without a clue there was a better way. I just did what I always did. It's all I knew. Sometimes in public service we hear these words of poor service delivery: "That's the way we've always done it." My hope is that it does not take you 50 years to embrace a new idea, concept, mindset, or method of serving.

A great tool to aid you in avoiding being in the dark is to embrace curiosity and be a life-long learner. Organizational psychologist Adam Grant says,

"Sticking to a single lane breeds stagnation. Carefully changing lanes is a path to growth." The internet is a powerful launch pad to growth, in that it offers many options for upping your skills game. In the way you learn best, be it visually or auditory, you can learn at your own pace. I am so appreciative of the way in which video content exists for everything these days, from Microsoft Office tips and tricks to visualizing data and presenting ideas; it's all readily available for you to add value to how and who you serve with excellence every day.

Another way to grow your skills is by reading. Read, read, and read some more. There are proven benefits to reading, but it complements your professional skills through improved vocabulary and communication skills. And guess what? It lowers stress. It's the trifecta of good reasons to do it. Again, reading is a simple yet worthwhile investment to ignite fulfilling, impactful service delivery every day.

Chapter 4

Full Cup Service

When we began our journey of what it means to serve with a Filled Cup, I shared with you the truth that public service is a high calling; it embodies honor, dignity, and most importantly excellence. We talked through the keys to breakthrough from the concept that serving others takes a Filled Cup, because just like a well without water is an empty hole in the ground, so, too, are you if you serve from an empty cup.

Full cup service is based on the 3Ps of The Filled Cup Framework of Person, Perspectives, and Professional Skills, and also requires awareness of potential cracks, chips, and fissures in our cup. We looked at alignment in our person — who we are and who we say we want to be — through our actions and interactions with those around us. We also considered with whom are we aligning ourselves - other people or someone greater, like Jesus. Then, we considered our mind which directs our emotions and how we react and interact with those around us. We also discussed the importance of asking for help if needed and listening to our spirit, that still, small voice of knowing right and wrong, and acting upon it for our own good and the good of others. When you are in alignment with who you are uniquely created to be in your body, mind, and spirit, you have the first component to serving fully.

We turned our attention to healthy perspectives, being grounded in the importance of the words we speak to ourselves and others, and the thoughts we entertain in our minds, as well as the content we consume. All of these have a profound impact on our views and, ultimately, our actions. The decisions we make and actions we take, especially when serving others, are tied to our perspectives. We make better decisions when we have a better perspective. Our perspectives benefit from comprehensive understanding of situations and peoples' emotions. We often have to fight against our biases and pre-existing beliefs to look at things differently. We have the opportunity to give the gift of grace when serving others by offering what is not deserved. It's important for us to choose a posture of humility over hubris. Our perspectives and position make up the second element of the framework.

Professional skills are the third side to the triangle of The Filled Cup Framework. You start with assessing your current technical skills, built by daily tasks, formalized training, and trial and error. You evaluate and improve your soft skills which are the ways in which you react to situations and interact with those around you. The critical concept related to professional skills is your willingness to lean into growth and not cling to your fixed mindset. Staying curious, pursuing life-long learning, and reading will accelerate your skills and enhance your value.

Meaningful public service that leaves a lasting impact is built upon the foundation of service with distinction; serving with distinction is noticeable every day. As you now know, the actionable framework to public service breakthrough that will set your service apart is The Filled Cup Framework based on the 3Ps: Person, Perspectives, and Professional Skills. What I have shared with you has the power to take you from ho-hum to humming in your adventures in public service. The choice is yours, but you have to decide to take action.

"You can't have transformation without application, or it's just information."
— Pedro Adao, Founder of 100X, 8-Figure
Entrepreneur, Bestselling Author

Knowledge is power, but applied knowledge is a superpower! If The Filled Cup Framework resonates with you and you aspire to answer the call to create fulfilling, lasting, impactful public service, head to www.TheFilledCup.info. At this website, get more information and sign up for a breakthrough clarity call with me to see if we are a good fit to go deeper into filling your cup.

The Filled Cup Self-Assessment

Give yourself a score from 1-5 for each 3P category below (1 being the lowest, 5 the highest). Bonus question amounts are added to your total score.

Assessment key is below.

Person
  Body   _____
  Emotions   _____
  Spirit   _____

Perspective
  Words   _____
  Content   _____
  Position   _____
  Grace   _____

Professional Skills
  Technical   _____
  Soft   _____

Person

Perspective   Professional Skills

Bonus:
Regularly read/listen to books or content? Add 4 points.
Occasionally read/listen to books or content? Add 2 points.

Filled Cup score _____

Full Cup, keep it up!	40-50 points
Half a cup, top it off!	25-39 points
You need a fill up!	< 24

No matter your score, head over to www.TheFilledCup.info for a free coaching strategy session. I want to help you in your journey to purpose and fulfillment.

About the Author

With over 15 years of serving in the public service sector, author Lisa Haley is currently a certified public finance (CPFO) professional serving in a leadership role as a financial management executive. Lisa is growing her coaching and mentorship business and pursuing certification as a 100X Kingdom Entrepreneur Coach to teach and mentor Kingdom entrepreneurs. She is on the Board of Virginia Women in Public Finance (VWPF) and is an active member of Women in Public Finance (WPF), the networking and educational association for public finance professionals. Along with having an MBA from George Mason University, Lisa enjoys road and gravel biking and lives with her husband and family in Ashburn, Virginia.

Are you looking for a guest expert for your podcast, team training, conference, or show?

Lisa has extensive leadership and mentoring experience in executive financial management, as well as public speaking. She has been a featured guest on the Unity Works Podcast and is available for keynote speeches and webinars with tailored content focusing on leadership and mentoring, as well as The Filled Cup Framework for public service excellence.

Lisa also offers a variety of 1:1 personal development coaching and mentoring services.

For more information please visit:
TheFilledCup.info

Are you in the honorable public service profession and desire to serve well, yet find yourself feeling underappreciated, unfulfilled, or lacking influence and true impact?

If you are anything like me, you are hardworking and dedicated, but find yourself sometimes going through the motions or just checking the box, not really making the difference you want to be making or living in your purpose. I have developed the public service industry's most transformative framework for next-level service excellence.

My immersive coaching experience will take you on a journey to breakthrough as you discover and implement next-level living and service. I want to partner with you and be your coach to help you achieve consistent service excellence.

If The Filled Cup and the 3P Framework resonates with you, head to www.TheFilledCup.info and click the link for a free strategy session to see if we are a good fit.

I look forward to hearing from you!

—Lisa Haley